STUDY GUIDE

Regina Swopes
Northeastern Illinois University

with
John Sisson

APPROACHING DEMOCRACY

FOURTH EDITION

Larry Berman
University of California at Davis

Bruce Allen Murphy
Lafayette College

Prentice Hall, Upper Saddle River, New Jersey 07458

© 2003 by PEARSON EDUCATION, INC.
Upper Saddle River, New Jersey 07458

ISBN 0-13-110257-5

Printed in the United States of America

Table of Contents

Chapter One

Approaching Democracy

Briefly define each of the following terms.

1. monarchy

2. democracy

3. theocracy

4. authoritarian regime

5. direct democracy

6. indirect democracy

7. town meeting

8. stability

9. minority rights

10. pluralism

Multiple Choice

11. The requirement that everyone must have the right to vote is called:

   a. democracy.
   b. electoral process.
   c. universal suffrage.
   d. representative government.

12. Which group was not allowed to vote when the Constitution was written?

   a. Women
   b. Native Americans
   c. African Americans
   d. All of the above

13. A system of government that allows indirect representation of the popular will is called:

   a. Pluralist.
   b. Populist.
   c. Republic.
   d. Theocracy.

14. All of the following are examples of democracy denied in America except the

   a. forced segregation and lack of voting rights of African Americans.
   b. forced internment of Japanese Americans during World War II.
   c. forced relocation of Native Americans.
   d. refusal to allow illegal aliens to enter the country.

15. The dissident student movement in 1989 that called itself "pro-democracy' and was crushed by its government occurred in

   a. China.
   b. Iran.
   c. the former Soviet Union.
   d. North Korea.

16. What feature of democracy was successfully used in the state of Colorado, when it passed an amendment banning state laws protecting gays and lesbians, only to have it overturned in federal?

    a. Equality   b. Majority rule
    c. Organized opposition   d. Self-government

17. All of the following would be examples of "freedom to" except

    a. the right to vote.
    b. the right to legal counsel.
    c. the right to equal protection under the law.
    d. the right to speak out against a political official.

18. The type of equality that would redistribute goods and services from the haves to the have-nots is called

    a. equality of relativity.   b. equality of opportunity.
    c. equality of results.   d. equality of establishment.

19. In a democratic system, a group becomes the majority by

    a. forcing people to adhere to the wishes of the group.
    b. persuading others to their side by popular input and rational argument.
    c. passing laws to prevent alternative rival groups from forming.
    d. All of the above.

20. Who is the final arbiter of the Constitution?

    a. The president   b. The Congress
    c. The Supreme Court   d. The states

True or False

21. T   F   In a democracy, voters designate a small number of people to represent their interests; those representatives then meet in a legislative body and make decisions on behalf of the entire citizenry.

22. T   F   Interest groups are temporary, informal organizations of government legislators.

23. T   F   An authoritarian regime is one in which government is apart from the people, oppressing the public by depriving them of basic civil and political liberties.

24. T F The framers chose representative rather than direct democracy because of the fear that pure democracy would mean rule by the mob.

25. T F Referenda are proposals submitted by the people of a state to the state's legislature for a vote.

26. T F Even though America has become more democratic than the framers envisioned, the basic structure of government they established still endures.

27. T F The reason the United States is said to be approaching democracy is that it has tried but fallen short of upholding core democratic values, such as freedom and equality.

28. T F The American military is controlled by the civilian government.

29. T F The unique power for the Supreme Court established in the case of Marbury v. Madison was original jurisdiction.

30. T F President Harry Truman was able to fire General Douglas MacArthur for insubordination during the Korean War due to the American tradition of a commitment to preserve freedom and equality.

Fill-in-the-Blanks

31. _____ _____ assumes that people can govern themselves.

32. A form of government that includes an annual meeting at which eligible citizens can express their views and cast votes is a _____.

33. Democracy in Athens emphasized face-to-face _____ _____ and decision making.

34. _____ _____ implies freedom from government intervention.

35. Every society, to be successful, must maintain _____ and provide social _____.

36. Continual competition among groups in a democracy ensures that power moves around in a _____ _____ of interests.

37. Groups known as Libertarian, Green, and Reform are all fairly recent _____ _____.

38. The institutions that most clearly allow people to influence government are _____.

39. The idea that government must stay out of the personal lives of citizens stems from the belief that we all have an inherent _____ ____ _____.

40. A _____ government, using the state to maintain total control over all citizens, suppresses open communication so as to maintain an iron grip over the minds of its populace.

Short Answer Essay

41. Describe the difference between equality of result and equality of opportunity.

42. Compare and contrast direct democracy with indirect democracy.

43. Describe a republican government.

44. Describe Athenian democracy.

45. List and discuss the core values of democracy.

46. Explain how liberty and equality can be contradictory.

47. What is the result of judicial review?

48. Explain how a concern for order and stability can conflict with freedom and equality.

49. Explain why and how democracies seek to balance majority rule with minority rights.

50. Describe the historical expansion of the democratic values of participation in America.

Chapter Two

The Founding and the Constitution

Briefly define each of the following terms

1. republic

2. sovereignty

3. limited government

4. The Sugar Act

5. The Townsend Revenue Acts

6. Committees of Correspondence

7. The Intolerable Acts

8.   Common Sense

9.   Declaration of Independence

10.   Virginia Plan

Multiple choice

11.   The proprietary colonies

    a.   were ones in which self-government was not allowed to exist.
    b.   were thinly disguised religious dictatorships.
    c.   were based on royal grants to an English nobleman who determined the nature of the colonial government.
    d.   quickly proved to be impractical and were transformed into independent entities.

12.   The most influential social contract theorist was

    a.   Thomas Hobbes.   b.   John Locke.
    c.   William Home.   d.   David Ricardo.

13.   The "elastic clause" that gives Congress some flexibility is called the:

    a.   Preamble
    b.   Necessary and Proper clause.
    c.   Enumeration clause.
    d.   Declaration of the Rights of Man.

14.   Among the major problems of the Articles of Confederation were all of the following, except

    a.   the national government could collect taxes.
    b.   the national government had no money to pay for an army.
    c.   the executive branch was too powerful.
    d.   the government could not enforce its laws.

15. Reserved powers are those given

    a.   to state governments.
    b.   exclusively to the federal government.
    c.   to both the states and federal governments.
    d.   only to local government.

16. What does the supremacy clause guaranty?

    a.   The supremacy of the legislative branch.
    b.   The supremacy of the federal government.
    c.   The supremacy of the Constitution over other laws and regulations.
    d.   The supremacy of interstate relations.

17. According to James Madison, the source of factions was

    a.   philosophical differences between elites and the masses.
    b.   the unequal divisions and types of property.
    c.   political parties and their respective leaders.
    d.   the repression of the minority by the ruling majority.

18. All of the following constitutional amendments had the purpose of expanding rights and equality, except the

    a.   Thirteenth Amendment.   b.   Fourteenth Amendment.
    c.   Eighteenth Amendment.   d.   Nineteenth Amendment.

19. The most recently added amendment to the Constitution deals with

    a.   granting the right to vote to 18 year olds.
    b.   the prohibition of poll taxes.
    c.   the granting of electoral votes to Washington D.C. residents.
    d.   the delay of congressional pay raises until the following session.

20. Which of the following nations has been most faithful in observing the principles contained in the U. S. Constitution?

    a.   India.   b.   China.
    c.   Japan.   d.   Hungary.

True or False

21.   T   F   The Mayflower Compact, signed on November 21, 1620 provided the basis for civil government.

22.   T   F   The United States has a unicameral legislature.

23. T   F   The notion of equality under the law was John Locke's most significant contribution to social contract theory.

24. T   F   The Intolerable Acts were passed by the British Parliament in response to Shays' Rebellion.

25. T   F   In a confederation, states defer to a central governing authority.

26. T   F   The success of the Constitutional Convention would have been impossible without a compromise on the slavery issue.

27. T   F   Vertical powers refer to the system of separation of powers among the three branches of the federal government.

28. T   F   The New Jersey Plan failed because it did not protect state powers.

29. T   F   The Antifederalists argued that the states should remain independent and distinct, rather than be led by a supreme national government.

30. T   F   The addition of a Bill of Rights to the Constitution was necessary for the document's ratification.

Fill-in-the-Blanks

31. A legislative system consisting of two houses or chambers is called a

_____.

32. The law-making branch of government is the _____.

33. A _____ _____ is a type of government in which the powers of the government are clearly defined and bounded, so that governmental authority cannot intrude in the lives of private citizens.

34. The _____ _____ _____ were a series of acts imposed by the British Parliament in 1767 on glass, lead, tea, and paper imported into the colonies.

35. The _____ _____ _____ were later replaced by the current constitution due to problems inherent in strong centralization.

36. _____ _____ theorists thought the most effective way to create the best government was to understand human nature in a state prior to government.

37. Using the _____ _____ _____ to select a person for the office of chief executive, each state gets one elector for each of its representatives and Senators.

38. The relationship between the centralized national government and the individual state governments is called _____.

39. The first ten amendments to the Constitution added in 1791 are known as the _____ _____ _____.

40. The Antifederalist party would later evolve into the _____ party.

Short Answer Essay

41. Explain the importance of Thomas Paine's *Common Sense*.

42. Describe the actions of the First Continental Congress and the Second Continental Congress.

43. Explain the concept of limited government.

44. Explain proportional representation.

45. Explain the causes of the American Revolution.

46. Describe the powers of Congress under the Articles of Confederation. Also explain some problems under the Articles of Confederation.

47. Describe the issues at the Constitutional Convention that divided the delegated and how they were finally resolved.

48. List the various checks that the branches of the national government can exercise on each other.

49. In your own words, explain the seven Articles of the Constitution.

50. Describe the differences between the Virginia Plan and the New Jersey Plan. What solution did the Connecticut Plan offer?

Chapter Three

Federalism

Briefly define each of the following terms.

1. federalism

2. inherent powers

3. McCullough v. Maryland

4. Gibbons v. Ogden

5. dual federalism

6. incorporation

7. conditions of aid

8. devolution revolution

9. federal mandates

10. New Federalism

Multiple Choice

11. All of the following would be examples of federalism in action, except

    a.   a state providing money for a state park system.
    b.   national funding for state and local police forces.
    c.   local floods leading to calls for national emergency assistance.
    d.   state and national funds being provided to build a road in a state.

12. The form of government in which all power is vested in a central government authority is called

    a.   federalism.
    b.   a unitary system.
    c.   a confederation.
    d.   None of the above.

13. The Social Security Act was implemented to provide economic security for those over the age of 65 and unemployment insurance. This demonstrates what advantage of federalism?

    a.   Policy diversity
    b.   Dispersal of power
    c.   Minimal policy conflict
    d.   Prospects for governmental experimentation

14. The triad of powers describes:

    a. federal, state and local cooperation
    b. the executive, legislative and judicial branches.
    c. The interstate commerce clause, the general welfare clause, and the Tenth Amendment.
    d. None of the above

15. Nullification was a nineteenth century concept that:

    a. the judiciary could overturn bad federal legislation.
    b. the federal government could overturn state laws
    c. the states could ignore other state laws.
    d. the states could ignore federal laws.

16. The primary way the general welfare clause has been used to expand national powers is through the national government

    a. directing operating anti-poverty programs.
    b. forcing state governments to operate the anti-poverty programs.
    c. regulating civil rights policies of state governments.
    d. giving money to states to operate programs according to national standards.

17. What powers are delegated specifically to the national government by the Constitution?

    a. Inherent powers
    b. Reserved powers
    c. Delegated powers
    d. Implied powers

18. The implied powers

    a. have been declared unconstitutional by the Supreme Court.
    b. are constricted to the states by the Fourth Amendment.
    c. can be inferred from delegated powers and justified by the elastic clause.
    d. are based on the power to ratify amendments to the Constitution.

19. The first major issue that caused conflict between national and state governments was the

    a. power to declare war against Britain.
    b. creation of a national bank.
    c. forced eviction of the eastern American Indians to west of the Mississippi River.
    d. purchase of the Louisiana Territory.

20. The view of federalism that holds each level as being supreme within its own jurisdiction is called

    a. dual federalism.
    b. creative federalism.
    c. exploratory federalism.
    d. rudimentary federalism.

True or False

21. T   F   The framers of the Constitution wanted to create a federal system that had clear, distinct, inflexible allocations of powers between the central and sate governments.

22. T   F   One of the advantages of federalism is that it can allow a great deal of diversity among policies and programs to accommodate the diverse population.

23. T   F   Implied powers are enumerated in the Consitition.

24. T   F   The general welfare clause has been used to protect state powers.

25. T   F   Cooperative federalism requires shared power and shared responsibility between local, state and federal governments.

26. T   F   Categorical grants are the most common grants-in-aid.

27. T   F   Although the intention of Nixon's general revenue sharing system was intended to return power to the states, the GRS in fact further extended the influence of the national government.

28.　T　　F　　The major goals of Carter's federalism proposals were to target funds to the areas with the greatest need and to encourage more private investment in social problems.

29.　T　　F　　The Supreme Court and lower court rulings have recently begun to redefine federalism in the direction of more state power.

30.　T　　F　　Conservative Republicans advocate a state-centered approach, arguing that solutions are best left either to state governments or to the private sector.

Fill-in-the-Blanks

31. The rights that have neither been granted to the national government nor forbidden to the states by the Constitution are called _____ _____.

32. The _____ _____ _____ is made up of three constitutional provisions that help to continually shift the balance of power between the national and state governments.

33. Congress used the _____ _____ _____ approach to achieve near uniformity on the new legal drinking age of twenty-one.

34. The _____ clause in the Article VI of the Constitution holds that in any conflict between federal laws and treaties and state laws, the will of the national government always prevails.

35. _____ _____ are those powers not assigned by the Constitution to the national government but left with the states or the people, according to the Tenth Amendment.

36. _____ _____ regulate health, morals, public safety, and welfare, which are reserved to the states.

37. A nineteenth-century theory which holds that states faced with unacceptable national legislation can declare such laws null and void and refuse to observe them is called

_____.

38. The process whereby the protections of the Bill of Rights have been found by the Supreme Court to apply to the states is called

_____.

39. A _____ _____ is a national requirement that must be observed.

40. A New Federalism program that allows multiple grants-in-aid for related policy areas can be consolidated into a single block grant is called _____ _____ _____.

Short Answer Essay

41. Describe the term concurrent powers. Please provide examples.

42. Explain the advantages and disadvantages of federalism.

43. Discuss how the interstate commerce clause has affected federalism.

44. Explain how the general welfare clause has affected federalism.

45. Discuss the impact of the Tenth Amendment upon federalism.

46. List those powers that the Constitution denies to both the national and state governments.

47. Discuss the importance of McCulloch v. Maryland.

48. Compare and contrast dual federalism with cooperative federalism.

49. Describe categorical, block, formula and project grants and the sorts of projects/policies each is used for.

50. Describe federalism under the current Bush administration.

Chapter Four

Congress

Briefly define each of the following terms.

1. bicameral legislature

2. reapportionment

3. gerrymandering

4. delegates

5. incumbents

6. franking privilege

7. term limits

8. "two congresses"

9. party caucus

10. minority leader

___

Multiple Choice

11. Congressional members are considered trustees when they:
   a. follow their best judgement.
   b. follow the lead of senior legislators in their party.
   c. bow to presidential influence.
   d. bow to pressure from their constituents.

12. In regard to representativeness,
   a. Congress is much more ethnically diverse than just a few decades ago.
   b. the membership of Congress accurately reflects America's different social groups.
   c. the Senate is much more representative of the variety of America's social groups than the House.
   d. wealthy representatives are unable to represent adequately the interests of the poor.

13. The size of the House of Representatives is
   a. established at 100 by the Constitution.
   b. established after each census and fluctuates between 400 and 500.
   c. set by legislation at 435.
   d. set by tradition to be four times the size of the Senate.

14. Representatives who would follow their constituents when voters have clear preferences and their own best judgement when the electorate is unsure are called

    a. brokers.   b. politicos.
    c. dynamos.   d. despots.

15. Incumbents have the following advantages, except

    a. financial.
    b. franking privilege.
    c. lack of voting record to defend.
    d. legislative experience.

16. Who is the president of the Senate?

    a. The president of the United States
    b. The Senate majority leader
    c. The Speaker of the House
    d. The vice president of the United States

17. What type of committee is formed to reconcile differences between the versions of a bill passed by the House and the Senate?

    a. Standing committee.   b. Select committee.
    c. Joint committee.   d. Conference committee.

18. The majority member with the longest continuous service in the Senate is the

    a. Senatoria maximus.   b. President pro tempore.
    c. President ante tempore.   d. None of the above.

19. A major difference between the House and Senate procedural rules is that:

    a. in the House, all amendments must be germane to the bill.
    b. in the Senate, all amendments must be germane to the bill.
    c. the House allows interest group representatives to speak on a bill before the floor.
    d. the Senate allows the president to give testimony to the Senate floor on the crucial bills.

20. Cloture requires approval of

    a. two-thirds of those present
    b. two-thirds of the entire Senate.
    c. three-fifths of the entire Senate.
    d. a simple majority of those present.

True or False

21. T F   House membership is more stable than that of the Senate.

22. T F   Congress has increased the ethnic diversity of its membership as a result of Supreme Court decisions and the redistricting that has taken place at the state level.

23. T F   A majority-minority district is one that has been redrawn in order to help keep incumbents in office.

24. T F   Representatives from marginal districts that could go either way electorally tend to vote according to personal opinion rather than constituency views.

25. T F   The advantage of incumbency is a relatively recent phenomenon.

26. T F   Congress as an institution has generally been held in high regard by the public.

27. T F   The position of president pro tempore is essentially honorary, carrying little political clout.

28. T F   Since both houses of congress jealously guard their independence and prerogatives, congress establishes only a few joint committees.

29. T F   The House is smaller, more decentralized, and more informal than the Senate.

30. T F   Presidential appointment of the House majority leader must be approved by the Senate.

Fill-in-the-Blanks

31.   The _____ _____ _____ clause of the Constitution, also called the elastic clause, has been interpreted by the Supreme Court to allow Congress to develop its role broadly with regard to regulating commerce, borrowing money, and collecting taxes.

32. A process of redrawing voting district lines from time to time and adjusting the number of representatives allotted each state is called _____.

33. Any attempt during the redistricting of congressional voting boundaries to create a safe seat for one party is called _____.

34. Congress members who feel authorized to use their best judgement in considering legislation see themselves a _____.

35. Individuals who currently hold public office are _____.

36. A legislated limit on the amount of time a political figure can serve in office is knows as _____ _____.

37. The American public's view of Congress has generally had a "Love my congressman, hate the Congress" view of the institution, know as the _____ _____ phenomenon.

38. Much of the legislative work of Congress is done is _____, the smaller work groups that consider and draft legislation.

39. When two opposing politicians support each other's legislation, the act of temporary alliance is called _____ _____.

40. When a member of Congress drafts and submits a piece of legislation dealing with a particular issue, that issue is said to be on the _____ _____.

Short Answer Essay

41. Explain why Congress is considered the world's most powerful legislature.

42. Describe the differences between membership in House of Representatives and membership in the Senate.

43. Describe the role of the Whip.

44. List the factors that limit Congress's power.

45. Describe the characteristics of those typically serving in Congress.

46. Explain how reapportionment, redistricting, and gerrymandering are related.

47. Describe the differences in the roles of delegate and trustee.

48. Explain the several advantages of incumbents over challengers in elections.

49. Describe the two different public views of Congress: as a legislative body and as individual members of Congress.

50. List the different types of committees in congress and give an example of each. Explain why Congress uses committees.

Chapter Five

The Presidency

Briefly define each of the following terms.

1. treaties

2. executive agreement

3. stewardship

4. constructionist

5. chief of staff

6. Executive Office of the President

7. cabinet

8. vice president

9. term limits

10. War Powers Resolution

Multiple Choice

11. The president has a fixed term of office, serving

    a. two years.   b. four years.
    c. six years.   d. three years.

12. Presidential is granted the Constitutional power to:

    a. veto congressional legislation.
    b. declare martial law during national emergencies.
    c. Both "a" and "b."
    d. None of the above.

13. Functional roles of the president include:

    a. Chief of State   b. United Nations Delegate
    c. Speaker of the Senate   d. None of the above.

14. Formal international agreements between sovereign states are called

    a. treaties.   b. lateral understandings.
    c. executive agreements.   d. joint resolutions of Congress.

15. What foreign policy tool did Theodore Roosevelt use to restrict Japanese immigration to the United States?

    a. Treaties   b. Executive agreements
    c. Lateral understandings   d. Joint resolutions of Congress

16. What is the most important specific power granted to the president by the Constitution?

    a. Veto power
    b. Executive privilege
    c. Appointment power
    d. Commander-in-Chief of the Armed Forces

17. What presidential role is illustrated in the president calling out the National Guard to lend assistance during natural disasters?

    a. Crisis leader
    c. Chief of state
    b. Chief diplomat
    d. Chief legislator

18. The president visits with leaders from other countries to maintain good relations with allies. This illustrates what presidential role?

    a. Chief of state
    c. Chief executive
    b. Chief diplomat
    d. Commander-in-chief

19. Which is a true statement about the War Powers Resolution?

    a. The Resolution's effectiveness at limiting presidential action has been proved by the historical record.
    b. The Resolution was passed over President Nixon's veto in 1973.
    c. The president does not have to consult Congress until some sixty days after she has ordered troops into combat overseas.
    d. None of the above.

20. The Brownlow Commission dealt with the issue of

    a. presidential war-making powers.
    b. permanent staffing for the president.
    c. improving communications between the president and the public.
    d. None of the above.

True or False

21. T F   The president has a central role in the legislative process through the power of the veto.

22. T F   The Constitution gives presidents the power to negotiate treaties with other nations.

23. T F   The enumerated power of executive privilege lets the president withhold his annual budget information from Congress

24. T F   Executive agreements allow presidents to make important foreign policy moves without Senate knowledge or approval.

25. T F   The Constitution makes no reference to party leadership.

26. T F   In comparison to domestic policy, presidents traditionally have great leeway and independence in their conduct of foreign policy.

27. T F   William Howard Taft's constructionist perspective believed the president's implied powers were limited.

28. T F   In the past few decades, it has become evident that a congressional declaration of war is no longer needed for a president to send American troops into combat.

29. T F   "Going public" is a strategy that recent presidents have scrupulously avoided.

30. T F   According to the Constitution, the president does not have a cabinet.

Fill-In-The-Blanks

31.   Under the Constitution, the selection of the president is made by the

_____ _____.

32.   Formal international agreements between sovereign states are called

_____.

33.   Diplomatic contracts negotiated with other countries that allow presidents to make important foreign policy moves without Senate approval are called _____ _____.

34.   The relationship between international crisis and presidential support has become know as the _____ _____

35.   A classic example of the _____ model of presidential power is illustrated in President Roosevelt's ordering the U.S. seizure of Panama and the subsequent building of the Panama Canal.

36. The view of presidential power espoused by William Howard Taft was the _____ view.

37. The _____ allows the president to forbid or prevent an action of Congress.

38. The _____ _____ _____ of 1973 requires that the president report to Congress within 48 houses after committing U. S. troops to hostile action.

39. The _____ _____ _____ is responsible for the operation of the White House, plays a key role in policy-making, and acts as gatekeeper to the president.

40. The _____ _____ is the second highest elected official in the United States.

Short Answer Essay

41. Describe the great paradox of the American presidency.

42. Describe the seven key principles upon which the framers based the presidency and the reasons behind them.

43. List and describe the formal powers given to the president in the Constitution.

44. List and describe the informal, or functional roles, of the president.

45. Explain the difference between the stewardship approach to executive power and the constructionist approach.

46. Explain why trends favor occupants of the White House being activist individuals.

47. Describe those factors that have resulted in the enlargement of presidential powers.

48. Describe presidential war powers.

49. Explain the role and function of the cabinet.

50. Describe the challenges of presidential leadership.

Chapter Six

The Judiciary

Briefly define each of the following terms.

1. original jurisdiction

2. Marbury v. Madison

3. statutory construction

4. trial court

5. criminal cases

6. class action suit

7. en blanc

8. docket

9. writ of certiorari

10. rule of four

Multiple Choice

11. The Supreme Court is the most undemocratic of the three branches because

    a. it operates in total secrecy.
    b. its justices are appointed rather than elected.
    c. the justices have almost total power to say what the law is.
    d. All of the above.

12. The authority of a court to hear a case after it has been argued and decided in a lower state or federal court is:

    a. Writ of Certiorari.   b. imminent domain.
    c. appellate jurisdiction.   d. Title V jurisdiction.

13. The power of the Court to interpret federal or state law and apply it to particular case is called

    a. literary exposition.   b. judicial imperialism.
    c. legal jurisprudence.   d. statutory construction.

14. What power is used most frequently by the Supreme Court?

    a. Judicial review
    b. Interpreting the meaning of a statue and applying it to a specific case
    c. Issuing writs of mandamus
    d. Refusing to review cases

15. All of the following points about appellate courts are true except

    a. usually appellate courts have multi-judge panels and no jury.
    b. appellate courts will consider only points of law.
    c. appellate courts will have additional witnesses and evidence to decide the guilt or innocence of the defendant.
    d. the ruling of appellate courts could lead to a new trial if they decide that the lower court had ruled incorrectly on points of law.

16. The doctrine that judges should adhere, if at all possible, to previously decided cases that are similar to the one under consideration is called

    a. "Let the decision stand."   b. following precedents.
    c. stare decisis.   d. All of the above.

17. What type of court is the U.S. Tax Court?

    a. Trial court   b. Appellate court
    c. Legislative court   d. District court

18. A decision of the Supreme Court that represents the agreed-upon compromise judgement of all the justices in the majority.

    a. majority-minority rule.   b. majority rule.
    c. majority opinion.   d. mandamus ruling.

19. Which of the following presidents have dramatically changed the direction of the Court?

    a. Kennedy   b. Nixon
    c. Reagan   d. All of the above.

20. The recent law school graduates who serve as assistants to Supreme Court Justices are called

    a. judicial fellows.   b. law apprentices.
    c. legal eagles.   d. law clerks.

True or False

21. T F   There is a strong correlation between judicial independence and democratic government.

22. T F   The appellate court considers only matters of law.

23. T F   Legislative court judges are appointed for life.

24. T F   Presidents tend to be bipartisan in their judicial appointments.

25. T F   If a Supreme Court appointment comes early in a president's term or during a period of presidential popularity, the Senate is more likely to allow a nomination to succeed.

26. T F   The Supreme Court never explains why it accepts or rejects cases.

27. T F   The judicial conference takes place in total secrecy, with only the justices present.

28. T F   A concurring opinion is one that a justice writes when she agrees strongly with the majority opnion and wants to reinforce the impact of their decision on society.

29. T F   Federal and state courts are supposed to follow Supreme Court precedents in making their own decisions.

30. T F   In actuality, Congress does not have any effective way to show discontent when the Supreme Court interprets a congressional action to ways Congress disapproves.

Fill-in-the-Blanks

31. When a court hears cases already argued and decided by another court, it has _____ jurisdiction.

32. The usual point of original entry into the legal system, with a single judge and jury deciding both fact and law, is called _____ court.

33. A _____ _____ suit is when two groups of people join together in a case in which the results will apply to all participants.

34. A procedure in which a president submits the names of judicial nominees to senators from the same political party, who are also from the nominee's home state, for their approval prior to formal nomination is called _____ _____.

35. The Supreme Court's agenda is called a _____.

36. In what is known as the _____ _____ _____, a vote by at least four justices to hear the case will grant the petition for a writ of certiorari and put the case on the Court's docket.

37. A written version of the decision of a court is the

_____.

38. When a justice disagrees with the holding of the court, frequently he or she will write a _____ _____, speaking for that justice alone or a few of the members of the Court.

39. A doctrine meaning "let the decision stand" is called _____

_____.

40. Judges who practice _____ _____ believe that they have a duty to reach out and decide issues even to the point, some critics charge, of writing their own personal values into law.

Short Answer Essay

41. Explain why the judicial branch of the national government was originally considered the least dangerous and why this view has changed.

42. List the constitutional provisions that were designed to keep the Supreme Court independent.

43. List ways in which the judiciary is influenced by outside forces.

44. Describe the organization of the federal courts.

45. Describe the process for appointing federal judges and the political factors that affect the appointment process.

46. Explain why the Senate has sought greater influence in the confirmation process and give the steps the president has taken to counteract this.

47. Describe how recent presidents have sought to leave their mark on the composition of the federal courts.

48. Give the factors the Court considers when selecting which cases to decide.

49. Give the reasons for the Court's shrinking docket.

50. Explain how the Supreme Court's decisions are implemented.

Chapter Seven

The Bureaucracy

Briefly define each of the following terms.

1. bureaucracy

2. specialization

3. formal rules

4. spoils system

5. Hatch Act

6. administrative discretion

7. regulation

8. independent agencies

9. government corporation

10. appointment power

Multiple Choice

11. Americans usually measure bureaucratic performance by

    a.   cost of service.
    b.   speed of delivery of service.
    c.   quality of the service compared to the private sector.
    d.   impact of bureaucratic failure.

12. People are concerned and suspicious about bureaucracy mainly because

    a.   it costs so much.
    b.   bureaucrats are so unrepresentative of the public.
    c.   it is hard to control bureaucracy and hold it accountable for its action.
    d.   there are so many obvious examples of failures to perform adequately.

13. The turning over of public responsibilities to privately owned and operated enterprises for regulation and for providing goods and services.

    a.   enterprise zoning.
    b.   business incubation.
    c.   publicity.
    d.   none of the above.

14. The bureaucracy performs all of the following governmental tasks, except

    a.   regulation.
    b.   centralization.
    c.   administration.
    d.   implementation.

15. A good example of federal bureaucratic regulation would be

    a. delivering the mail.
    b. collecting entry fees from each international airline passenger.
    c. building and flying the space shuttle.
    d. enforcing the anti-discriminatory guidelines of the Equal Employment Opportunity commission.

16. A clear chain of communication and command running from an executive director through all levels of workers is called:

    a. hierarchy.
    b. hegemony.
    c. group maintenance.
    d. None of the above.

17. Among the constraints on bureaucratic behavior are all of the following, except

    a. bureaucratic agencies do not control their own revenue.
    b. the rules as to how to deliver services are established elsewhere.
    c. bureaucratic goals are mandated by other units of government.
    d. the heads of most bureaucratic agencies are publicly elected.

18. The friendly, interdependent relationship between Congress and certain federal agencies is called the

    a. devil's duo.
    b. cozy coterie.
    c. iron triangle.
    d. steel magnolia.

19. The agency that is the nation's chief covert operations and information gathering bureau is the

    a. National Security Agency.
    b. State Department Councillor Service.
    c. Central Intelligence Agency.
    d. Bureau of External Intelligence Resource.

20. What is the excessive amount of rules and regulations that government employees must follow called?

    a. Red tape.
    b. Iron law.
    c. Multiplicity of agents.
    d. Spoils system.

True or False

21. T F   Although New Deal programs were designed as temporary emergency programs to relieve the suffering of the Depression, most agencies became a permanent part of an enlarged federal bureaucracy.

22. T F   The great majority of federal employees work in or near the national capital, Washington, D.C.

23. T F   The routine task performed by bureaucrats to achieve a specific policy goal is called administration.

24. T F   Federal bureaucratic agencies are actually more a part of the legislative branch than of the executive.

25. T F   Independent agencies are usually smaller than cabinet departments and have a narrower set of responsibilities.

26. T F   Cabinet departments are major administrative units whose heads are presidential advisers appointed by the president and confirmed by the Senate.

27. T F   C-SPAN is an issue network.

28. T F   Congress does not allow agencies to keep money left over when the fiscal year ends.

29. T F   Privatization involves securing the confidentiality of government records on individual private citizens.

30 . T F   Bureaucratic organizations are inherently undemocratic.

Fill-in-the-Blanks

31. _____ _____ _____ were established to regulate a sector of the nation's economy in the public interest.

32. In a bureaucracy, _____ _____ govern the execution of all tasks within the jurisdiction of a given agency.

33. The _____ _____ is a social system whereby the government assumes primary responsibility for the welfare of citizens.

34. A system in which government jobs and contracts are awarded on the basis of party loyalty rather than social or economic status of relevant experience is called the _____ _____.

35. The system of hiring and promoting employees based on professional merit is called _____ _____.

36. _____ is the actual execution of a policy.

37. Major administrative units whose heads are presidential advisers appointed by the president and confirmed by the Senate are _____ _____.

38. The informal three-way relationships that develop among key legislative committees, the bureaucracy whose budgets are supervised by those committees, and interest groups with a vested interest in the policies created by those committees and agencies are called _____ _____.

39. The Civil Service Reform Act of 1978 created the _____ _____ _____, a group of upper-management bureaucrats with access to private-sector incentives such as bonuses but also subject to measurable job-performance evaluations.

40. The administrative unit in the Executive Office of the President whose main responsibilities are to prepare and administer the president's annual budget is the _____ of _____ & _____.

Short answer essay

41. Describe bureaucracy and explain three ways that a bureaucracy promotes efficiency.

42. Describe the problems inherent in bureaucratic form.

43. Explain the purpose of the Hatch Act and how it has been amended in recent years.

44. List and describe the three key government tasks performed by the bureaucracy.

45. List and briefly describe the four government institutions that constitute the federal bureaucracy.

46. Describe how presidents may control the bureaucracy.

47. Describe how Congress may control the bureaucracy.

48. Describe some problems associated with the FBI and the CIA.

49. Explain and evaluate the common criticisms of the government bureaucracy.

50. List several reforms that have been proposed for the federal bureaucracy, then explain the results of each.

Chapter Eight

Public Opinion

Briefly define each of the following terms.

1. public opinion

2. respective sampling

3. gender gap

4. political culture

5. political ideology

6. culture theory

7. schemas

8. realignment

9. intensity

10. latency

Multiple Choice

11. James Madison would argue that

    a.   public opinion should always be heeded.
    b.   public opinion should always be totally ignored.
    c.   public opinion should be taken into account, but not followed slavishly.
    d.   None of the above.

12. In a random sample

    a.   every member of the population must have an equal chance of appearing in the sample.
    b.   only men should be questioned.
    c.   only women should be questioned.
    d.   only voters should be questioned.

13. Close-knit families produce offspring whose political views

    a.   are very similar.
    b.   are very diverse.
    c.   are extremely conservative.
    d.   are extremely liberal.

14. The issue of school prayer in public schools

    a.   has never been an issue in the United States.
    b.   is only important to Muslims.
    c.   is highly controversial.
    d.   has been resolved.

15. The effect of social class upon political views

    a.   has always been clear.
    b.   has proven very difficult to measure.
    c.   has changed throughout history.
    d.   has only been measured in Canada.

16. In general, minorities

    a.   distrust society and public authorities.
    b.   often feel alienated from society.
    c.   vote less frequently than those in the majority.
    d.   All of the above.

17. Political socialization:

    a.   begins in childhood.
    b.   may be influenced by a person's gender.
    c.   comes from the media
    d.   All of the above.

18. Which is America's most conservative region?

    a.   The South.   b.   The Northeast.
    c.   The Midwest.   d.   Florida.

19. As a well-informed citizenry, Americans

    a.   are about average for democracies.
    b.   fall short.
    c.   are up to par on some issues, and totally ignorant on others.
    d.   are very well versed on public issues.

20. Party identification

    a.   is still very strong in America.
    b.   is a good predictor of an individual's political behavior.
    c.   determine how a political candidate is evaluated.
    d.   None of the above.

True or False

21. T   F   It is generally held that no president can respond to every change in public opinion.

22. T   F   Opinion polls are not an important aspect of American politics.

23. T   F   In political polls, a random sample includes members of only one political party.

24. T   F   Hispanics tend to vote overwhelmingly Republican.

25. T   F   Generational patterns show that people who grow up during certain periods often share similar political and social outlooks. These outlooks differ from one generation to the next.

26. T   F   People living in rural areas are generally more conservative.

27. T   F   The gender gap refers to the difference in political opinions between men and women.

28. T   F   One of the core values of American society is political inequality.

29. T   F   Many Americans do not identify themselves as either liberal or conservative.

30. T   F   An issue is salient if people do not think it affects them.

Fill-in-the-Blanks

31.   The main problem with most polls is that they fail to achieve a
_____ _____.

32.   Attention to _____ _____ is important for reliable results.

33.   _____ _____ are used by the media to trace the support levels of candidates over time.

34.   A non-scientific poll that assesses public opinion is known as
_____.

35.   More than anything else, _____ has emerged to dominate the social and political landscape.

36. Generally, the more religious one is the more _____ one tends to be.

37. The leading American value is _____.

38. _____ _____ is a coherent way of viewing politics and government.

39. A _____ is an intellectual framework for evaluating the world.

40. _____ is a measure of the depth of feeling associated with a given opinion.

Short Answer Essays

41. Describe sampling bias and margin of error.

42. Describe the different types of public opinion polls -- straw, tracking, and exit. Which is the most accurate? Which has the biggest potential for affecting the outcome of a political race?

43. What are the major factors involved in measuring public opinion?

44. List the major institutions of political socialization and the contribution of each.

45. List and discuss the core values of America's political culture.

46. What are the major political ideologies in America?

47. Discuss how politically aware and involved most Americans are.

48. What is the relationship between public opinion and public policy?

49. Discuss the uses of public opinion in Middle Eastern countries:

50. Describe current public opinion on the death penalty and how the government has responded to that public opinion.

Chapter Nine

Political Parties

Briefly define each of the following terms.

1. political parties

2. realignment

3. King Caucus

4. New Deal coalition

5. local party organization

6. machine politics

7. national party convention

8. nomination

9. primary election

10. proportional representation

Multiple Choice

11. A nongovernmental institution that organizes and gives direction to mass political desires in the pursuit of power is called a(n)

    a.   interest group.
    c.   think tank.
    b.   mass media organization.
    d.   political party.

12. A significant historical event that causes major shifts in party identification and loyalty is called

    a.   party realignment.
    c.   party amalgamation.
    b.   party reduction.
    d.   bipartisan cooperation.

13. The tendency of most party primaries and caucuses to be held early in the nomination schedule to lock up delegate support early is called

    a.   lead dogging.
    c.   front loading.
    b.   early birding.
    d.   log rolling.

14. A statement of principles, policies and goals a party pledges to carry out if voters give it control of the government is called

    a.   party caucus
    c.   party identification.
    b.   party platform.
    d.   None of the above.

15. What is the most basic role of parties?

    a.   To raise money for party employees.
    b.   To nominate candidates and win elections.
    c.   To offer comfort to people confused by the political process.
    d.   To fight for ideologically distinct policy preferences.

16. In trying to find out what voters want and giving it to them, parties are carrying out their

   a. representation function.   b. inductive function.
   c. demagogic function.   d. least important function.

17. The major task of the national party organization is to

   a. organize the national party conventions every four years.
   b. select the presidential and vice presidential candidates every four years.
   c. draft the party platform that all party nominees must pledge to support.
   d. All of the above.

18. Meetings of party adherents who gather to discuss and deliberate, and then give their support to a candidate for president are called

   a. caucuses.   b. open primaries.
   c. closed primaries.   d. blanket primaries.

19. What type of primary allows cross-party voting?

   a. Open primary.   b. Closed primary.
   c. Caucus.   d. Blanket primary.

20. The single-member district electoral system inhibits the development of

   a. third parties.   b. interest groups.
   c. coalitions.   d. political action committees.

True or False

21. T   F   Political parties are not mentioned in the Constitution.

22. T   F   Today's Democratic party, a direct descendant of Jefferson's party, is the oldest political party in the world.

23. T   F   Where parties are weak, interest groups are strong.

24. T   F   Party activists are wealthier and better educated than the population at large.

25. T   F   The Democrats are more effective at fund-raising than the Republicans.

26. T F   Americans have tended to prefer primary elections, which are more inclusive and democratic in nature than caucuses.

27. T F   The open primary is used by most states.

28. T F   A caucus is a meeting of party adherents to select delegates.

29. T F   Political Action Committees monitor election fairness and fraud.

30. T F   Interest groups have recently declined in their influence.

Fill-in-the-Blanks

31.   Nongovernmental institutions that organize and give direction to mass political desires are called _____.

32.   The first election in the world in which one party (the Federalist party of John Adams) willingly gave up power because of a lost election to another party (the Republican party of Thomas Jefferson) without bloodshed was called the _____.

33.   _____ is the process by which parties look for effective, popular candidates to help them win votes and offices.

34.   The _____ is a system of nominating candidates in which voters in each state make the choice by casting ballots.

35.   An organizational style of local politics in which party bosses traded jobs, money, and favors for votes and campaign support was called

_____.

36.   The _____ is the statement of principles and policies, the goals that a party pledges to carry out if voters give it control of the government.

37. In the _____ system, the winner of the primary or electoral college vote gets all of the state's convention or electoral college delegates.

38. In the _____ primary, only citizens registered as members of a particular political party may participate in that party's primary.

39. Delegates to the Democratic National Convention who are not bound to vote for any particular candidate are called _____.

40. The group of 538 electors who meet separately in each of their states and the District of Columbia on the first Monday following the second Wednesday in the December after a national presidential election to officially elect the president and the vice president of the United States are called the _____.

Short Answer Essay

41. Describe the functions political parties perform.

42. Give a brief description of the five party systems.

43. Give the evidence for and against the assertion that there was a 6th realignment after 1968.

44. List and explain why the United States has a two-party system.

45. Explain why minor parties appear, and describe their performance. Historically, what have been some of the functions of minor parties?

46. Describe the various levels of party organization.

47. Give five reasons why the old machine systems of politics declined during the 20th century.

48. Describe the process by which a Democrat or a Republican becomes a candidate for president.

49. Discuss the various attempts to reform the nomination process since 1968.

50. Discuss party identification over the course of American history. How important is it in modern elections?

Chapter Ten

Participation, Voting, and Elections

Briefly define each of following terms

1. voter turnout

2. retrospective voting

3. protest

4. political violence

5. midterm elections

6. coattail effect

7. faithless elector

8. contingency election

9. federal matching funds

10. soft money

Multiple Choice

11. Reviewing the participation levels of Americans, one can conclude that

    a.   very few Americans are active to any degree in politics.
    b.   close to half of the population is engaged in some form of serious, politically oriented activity.
    c.   nearly all Americans are active participants in political life.
    d.   None of the above.

12. Many political observers measure the health of a democracy by the degree to which citizens participate in elections. This is referred to as

    a.   voter turnout.   b.   voter pullover.
    c.   voter mobility.   d.   electoral responsiveness rate.

13. The process of campaigning to persuade the public to take a position on an issue is

    a.   issue networking.   b.   issue advocacy.
    c.   issue staging.   d.   None of the above.

14. Mass political involvement through voting and campaign work and many other activities is called:

    a.   participation.   b.   socialization.
    c.   canvassing.   d.   muckraking.

15. A major new way of organizing political events is

    a.   two-way closed circuit television.
    b.   forming highly organized cells, much like the old communist party did.
    c.   electronic mail and the Internet.
    d.   personal columns in daily newspapers.

16. The 1998 election was called a

    a. contingency election.   b. maintaining election.
    c. midterm election.   d. presidential election.

17. To be officially elected president one must

    a. receive a majority of the total electoral college votes.
    b. have both the highest popular vote total and win a majority of the total electoral college votes.
    c. win a majority in a congressional vote of confidence and investiture.
    d. win a plurality of total electoral college votes.

18. How many electoral votes does a winning candidate need to receive the required majority?

    a. 50   b. 200
    c. 270   d. 538

19. The major strategy in a presidential campaign is

    a. raising the most money possible for a television commercial blitz.
    b. not alienating any vital voter group.
    c. going where the votes are, to the big states.
    d. adhering to every Federal Election Commission rule in order to avoid decertification.

20. What are independent expenditures?

    a. Funds spent by independent candidates or minor parties
    b. Funds a candidate spends to cover the costs of fund-raising
    c. Funds now outlawed by a recent Supreme Court ruling
    d. Funds spent by a group for a cause and not coordinated with a candidate.

True or False

21. T F   The U.S. Supreme Court has ruled that the motor-voter law was an infringement on the states right to govern.

22. T F   Political activists are largely well-educated, middle and upper-income white voters.

23. T F   The United States has the highest level of voter turnout among all democratic countries.

24. T F   Younger people are more likely to vote than older people.

25. T F   Initiatives are submitted by a state legislature to the public for popular vote.

26. T F   Civil disobedience is violent by definition.

27. T F   When the popular vote and electoral college votes differ on the winner of a presidential race, it's called a deviating election.

28. T F   To become president, the winning candidate must receive 270 of the 538 electoral votes.

29. T F   Only about 55 percent of the electorate turn out to vote for president.

30. T F   Regional realignment has occurred in the South, particularly among males who formerly supported the Republican party and now are solidly Democrats.

Fill-in-the-Blanks

31. One technique designed to keep African Americans from voting was the _____, a fee that had to be paid before one could vote.

32. The percentage of eligible voters who actually show up and vote on election day is referred to as _____.

33. An _____ is a proposal submitted by the public and voted upon during elections.

34. Ballots on which people vote for candidates of only one party are called _____ tickets.

35. A powerful form of issue voting in which voters look back over the last term or two to judge how well an incumbent or the in party has performed in office is called _____.

36. Elections in which Americans elect members of Congress but not presidents are called _____.

37. A member of the electoral college who casts his or her vote for someone other than the states popular voter winner is called the

_____.

38. An election in which the majority party of the day wins both Congress and the White House is called a _____ election.

39. Contributions used by state and local party organizations for party building activities are called _____.

40. A loophole in the campaign finance law involving no limits to funds that are dispersed independently by a group or person in the name of a cause, presumably not by a candidate, involves _____.

Short Answer Essay

41. Describe the different amounts of political participation in the U.S..

42. List the steps taken to keep blacks from voting after passage of the Fifteenth Amendment.

43. Describe the different levels of voter turnout in congressional and presidential elections.

44. What are some of the explanations for poor turnout in U.S. elections? Give some of the institutional and psychological explanations for why Americans do not register to vote.

45. Define initiative and referendum and describe how successful each has been.

46. Identify the factors that must be present for issue voting to occur.

47. Describe ways of participating in politics other than voting.

48. Give the reasons for the framers designing the electoral college. Compare its original design with how the electoral college works today.

49. Give the proposals for reforming the electoral college and the pros and cons of each proposal.

50. Over the years, campaign reform efforts have sought to limit the influence of money on elections. Describe some of those reforms and their successes and failures.

Chapter Eleven

Interest Groups

Briefly define each of the following terms.

1. interest groups

2. policy entrepreneur

3. political action committees

4. collective action

5. free riders

6. lobbying

7. grass-roots activity

8. soft money

9. gridlock

10. policy networks

Multiple Choice

11. Americans have long been noted for their propensity to

a. wage war.
c. join groups.

b. participate in elections.
d. None of the above.

12. Interest groups that have already been formed are called

a. potential groups.
c. actual groups

b. active groups.
d. policy initiators.

13. Which of the following would not be considered a liberal group?

a. The American Civil Liberties Union
b. The National Organization of Women
c. The National Rifle Association
d. The National Association for the Advancement of Colored People

14. The information provided by interest groups tends to be

a. biased.
c. primarily religious in nature.

b. totally wrong.
d. None of the above.

15. The United States Chamber of Commerce has an annual budget of

a. 10 million dollars.
c. 65 million dollars.

b. 20 million dollars.
d. 129 million dollars.

16. Religious groups are a type of

    a. civil rights group.
    b. ideological group.
    c. business group.
    d. All of the above.

17. Interest groups that have no actual substantive form -- and may never have one -- but could come into being and affect political discourse are called

    a. actual groups.
    b. business groups.
    c. single issue groups.
    d. None of the above.

18. Members who do not invest but still share in the collective benefits of group action are know as

    a. free riders.
    b. loafers.
    c. leaders.
    d. None of the above.

19. The first political action committee was created in

    a. 1980.
    b. 1974.
    c. 1972.
    d. 1948.

20. Interest group activity is protected by the

    a. Second Amendment.
    b. Tenth Amendment.
    c. Nineteenth Amendment.
    d. First Amendment.

True or False

21. T F   Soft money was banned from federal elections after the November 2002 elections.

22. T F   Madison believed that interest group activity was a logical consequence of human nature.

23. T F   There were no interest groups in the U.S. prior to 1980.

24. T F   Interest groups are primarily concerned with the poor and disadvantaged.

25. T F   The most common type of groups are business groups.

26. T F   The book *Unsafe At Any Speed* was authored by 2000 presidential candidate Al Gore.

27. T   F   Interest groups want to be government, not merely influence government.

28. T   F   Interest group leaders spend a great deal of time engaged in group maintenance.

29. T   F   Today there are fewer than 1500 lobbyists.

30. T   F   Interest group lobbying is limited to Congress.

Fill-in-the-Blanks

31. Madison believed that the power of actions could be moderated by _____ their influence.

32. People form and join groups because _____ _____ is stronger, more credible, and more likely to influence policy outcomes than the isolated actions of individuals.

33. One of the most interesting developments in American government since the 1960s is the dramatic increase in _____

_____ _____.

34. _____ _____ interest groups are organizations that represent citizens who are primarily concerned with one particular policy or social problem.

35. Group leaders must devote a major portion of their time to _____

_____.

36. For lobbyists, _____ is crucial.

37. Groups use _____ _____ to target citizens with mailings describing the group's cause.

38. _____ is the formal, organized attempt to influence legislation.

39. Campaign contribution directed to advancing the interests of a political party or an issue in general, rather than a specific candidate is called _____ _____.

40. Political scientist _____ _____ argued that interest groups played a stabilizing role in American politics.

Short Answer Essays

41. What is the difference between an actual group and a potential group? Which group can politicians ignore?

42. List some of the functions interest groups perform, and provide a recent example from the news.

43. List the different types of interest groups. Give a modern example of each.

44. Describe the factors that influence the development of interest groups.

45. Discuss the free-rider problem.

46. Give the various differences in interest groups that help explain their different levels of success.

47. How may corporate scandals, like the collapse of Enron, have affected lobbying?

48. Discuss results of the 2002 elections and the role of interest groups in those elections.

49. Explain the growth of political action committees (PACs), and discuss the problems associated with them.

50. Explain the use of Web sites and the internet as lobbying tools. How effective may they be vs. more traditional forms of lobbying?

Chapter Twelve

The Media

Briefly define each of the following terms.

1. spin

2. muckraking

3. yellow journalism

4. socialization

5. Federal Communications Commission

6. fairness doctrine

7. right of rebuttal

8. prior restraint

9. libel

10. "narrowcasting"

Multiple Choice

11. The job of the media is to

    a.   transmit information.
    b.   simplify complex details into symbols and images.
    c.   Both of the above.
    d.   Neither of the above.

12. The term "yellow journalism" is derived from

    a.   a type a paper used to publish newspapers.
    b.   lurid, illustrated news accounts associated with
          Hearst and Pulitzer newspapers.
    c.   news stories which occur in the late evenings.
    d.   newspapers with a yellow mark on the front.

13. The equal time rule specifies that:

    a.   Candidates must be allowed equal time on radio and television.
    b.   Candidates must be allowed equal time on radio and television, as well
          as equal coverage in newspapers and magazines.
    c.   In televised debates, candidates must be given equal time
          to address the same issues.
    d.   None of the above.

14. Social scientists generally agree that the mass media perform which of the following functions?

   a. Surveillance of world events
   b. Interpretation of events
   c. Socialization of individuals into cultural settings
   d. All of the above.

15. Investigative journalism is different from yellow journalism in

   a. the amount of time spent on a particular story.
   b. investigative journalists are paid more money.
   c. newspapers which feature yellow journalism are sold only in grocery stores.
   d. Investigative journalism makes greater use of technology.

16. Speech that is untruthful, malicious, or damaging to a person's reputation or good name and thus not protected the First Amendment is called

   a. libel.
   b. slander.
   c. fighting words.
   d. hate speech.

17. Which of the following is not a guideline which the electronic media must follow?

   a. A rule limiting the number of stations an individual or organization may own
   b. A rule mandating public-service programing
   c. A rule that older journalists must be paid more than younger journalists
   d. A rule promising to protect the rights of individuals

18. During presidential campaigns the media tends to focus on

   a. the issues.
   b. the election rules.
   c. the candidates.
   d. the voters.

19. Which of the following would not be done by a candidate attempting to counter negative advertising?

   a. Defending against the charges
   b. Attacking the credibility of the accuser
   c. Ignoring the attack
   d. Quitting the race

20. The most successful use of radio by a politician was

    a.   Nixon's "Checkers Speech."
    b.   Roosevelt's "Fireside Chats."
    c.   Clinton's "Weekly Address."
    d.   Lincoln's "Gettysburg Address."

True or False

21. T F   Democracy requires that most governmental activities be kept secret.

22. T F   The term spin derives from sports.

23. T F   Newspapers were not widely read until the 1980's.

24. T F   Television coverage of new events tends to be very slow.

25. T F   The term narrowcasting was coined by Edward R. Murrow.

26. T F   The media never interprets the news, they only report.

27. T F   There is a correlation between exposure to mass media and a person's fear of violent crime.

28. T F   The media is protected by the Fifteenth Amendment.

29. T F   Opinion polls are rarely used these days.

30. T F   There is no evidence that the media significantly affects public opinion.

Fill-in-the-Blank

31.   The right to refute allegations presented on radio or TV within a reasonable time is the _____ _____ _____.

32.   The most widely read news magazine is _____.

33.   The sprit of the muckraker can still be seen in the practice of

     _____ _____.

34. The media plays an important role in the process by which people learn to conform to the society's norms and values. This is called

    _____.

35. Functions of the media include _____, _____,

    _____, and _____.

36. The _____ _____, now abandoned, required radio and television stations to provide a reasonable percentage of time for programs dealing with issues of public interest.

37. Governmental suppression of information is known as _____

    _____.

38. The relationship between the media and the government is often termed as _____.

39. The media has been accused of focusing on the _____ _____ nature of politics.

40. Over the years _____ have become progressively shorter.

Short Answer Essays

41. Discuss the controversy over the proper relationship between the media and democracy. Is it really symbiotic? If so, should it be?

42. Trace the recent evolution of technology and the mass media in America.

43. What have been some of the consequences of new technology on the media, its audience, and the coverage of public policy.

44. What has been the impact of talk radio during the past decade?

45. Describe the functions of the mass media, including surveillance, interpretation, investigative journalism, and socialization.

46. In which functions does the media take a more adversarial role towards the government? In which functions does it take on a cooperative role?

47. Describe how the Federal Communications Commission regulates the media.

48. Discuss some of the limits placed on the mass media, as well as some protections it enjoys, such as freedom from prior restraint.

49. How can a candidate counter negative advertising?

50. Discuss the media's role in the election process.

Chapter Thirteen

Civil Liberties

Briefly define each of the following terms.

1. civil liberties

2. civil rights

3. clear and present danger test

4. double jeopardy

5. Lemon test

6. secular regulation rule

7. least restrictive means test

8. fighting words

9. prior restraint

10. subsequent punishment

Multiple Choice

11. Civil liberties are guaranteed by

    a.   state laws.
    b.   some state constitutions.
    c.   the Bill of Rights and the due process clause of the Fourteenth Amendment.
    d.   the Seventh Amendment.

12. Cases involving civil liberties nearly always come down to conflict between the

    a.   church and state.
    b.   individual and state.
    c.   corporation and individuals.
    d.   local government and federal government.

13. Probable cause is related to which constitutional protection?

    a.   free speech
    b.   right to assemble peaceably
    c.   guarantee from unreasonable search and seizure
    d.   freedom of religion

14. The clear and present danger doctrine of Justice Holmes

    a.   states that the circumstances and nature of speech could justify its restriction.

    b.   was applied to cases involving speech that might hinder the war effort.

    c.   was later abandoned by Holmes.

    d.   All of the above.

15. The exclusionary rule refers to:

    a.   police evidence.

    b.   discrimination based on race.

    c.   the right to legal counsel.

    d.   None of the above.

16. Some actions, such as burning the American flag, take the place of speech and are commonly called

    a.   substitute speech.   b.   hate speech.

    c.   symbolic speech.   d.   fighting words.

17. What amendment provides for the right to be represented by counsel?

    a.   Fourth Amendment   b.   Fifth Amendment

    c.   Sixth Amendment   d.   Eighth Amendment

18. In *Katz v. United States*, the scope of the Fourth Amendment was extended to include

    a.   police searches.   b.   grand jury testimony.

    c.   electronic eavesdropping.   d.   double jeopardy.

19. The Fifth Amendment includes all of the following, except the

    a.   right not to be compelled to be a witness against yourself in a criminal trial.

    b.   protection against double jeopardy.

    c.   protections against cruel and unusual punishment.

    d.   right to a speedy and public trial by an impartial jury.

20. According to the text, the right to obtain an abortion:

    a.   is likely to be overturned soon by the Court.

    b.   appears to be secure with the current composition of the Court.

    c.   is not considered a binding precedent by the current Court.

    d.   will disappear with the next Supreme Court appointment.

True or False

21. T   F   The Supreme Court has ruled that flag-burning is protected as symbolic speech.

22. T   F   Civil rights are derived largely from the Bill of Rights and the due process clause of the Fourteenth Amendment.

23. T   F   Cases involving civil liberties almost always derive from a conflict between the individual and the state.

24. T   F   The Supreme Court has ruled that slander and libel are protected by the First Amendment.

25. T   F   Gag orders barring the media from publishing information about an ongoing criminal case are very common today.

26. T   F   As it stands now, the Supreme Court will not allow attempts to regulate alleged pornography on the Internet.

27. T   F   Loopholes in the exclusionary rule, such as the good faith exception, seriously weaken the guarantee of privacy implied in the Fourth Amendment.

28. T   F   Prisoners on death row are disproportionately black, and almost all are male.

29. T   F   The right of privacy is not explicitly mentioned in the Constitution.

30. T   F   It is difficult to legally define obscenity.

Fill-in-the-Blanks

31. The approach in which the Bill of Rights would be absorbed into the due process clause by the simple act of redefinition was called the _____ of the Bill of Rights.

32. A free speech test allowing states to regulate only speech that has an immediate   connection to an action states are permitted to regulate is called the _____.

33. Being tried twice for the same crime is called _____ and is banned by the Fifth Amendment.

34. The _____ test emerged from the Supreme Court case Lemon v. Kurtzman in 1971.

35. The _____ rule holds that there is no constitutional right to exemption, on free exercise grounds, from laws dealing with nonreligious matters.

36. Certain expressions are so volatile that they are deemed to incite injury. They are not protected under the First Amendment and are thus referred to as _____.

37. Speech or symbolic actions intended to inflict emotional distress, defame, or intimidate people is called _____.

38. _____, such as burning the American flag, takes the place of speech because they communicate a message.

39. _____ is an action in which the government seeks to ban the publication of controversial material by the press before it is published.

40. The _____ warning must be recited by police officers to a suspect before questioning.

Short Answer Essay

41.   How have the "War on Drugs" and "War on Terrorism" affected civil liberties and civil rights?

42.   Explain how the civil liberties protections in the Bill of Rights were applied to states.

43.   Describe how the U.S.A. Patriot Act may encroach on constitutionally protected liberties. How is this related to the "clear and present danger" test?

44.   Explain the different forms of incorporation, including no incorporation, partial incorporation, selective incorporation, and total incorporation.

45.   Describe how the Supreme Court has decided "establishment of religion" cases.

46. Describe how the Supreme Court has decided
"free exercise of religion" cases.

47. Describe the how the Constitution defines "unreasonable searches and
seizures" and modern Supreme Court rulings on this protection.

48. Describe the Court's rulings in the area of freedom of the press.

49. Explain the Court's view on the right to privacy.

50. How does the Supreme Court decide what is and isn't obscene?

Chapter Fourteen

Civil Rights and Political Equality

Briefly define each of the following terms.

1. discrimination

2. black codes

3. suffrage

4. state action

5. peonage

6. civil disobedience

7. boycott

8. affirmative action

9. test of reasonableness

10. equality

Multiple Choice

11. All of the following were federal actions before the Civil War to protect slavery in some way, except the

    a.   Wilmot Proviso.
    b.   Fugitive Slave Act.
    c.   Missouri Compromise.
    d.   Compromise of 1850.

12. In the Dred Scott case, the Supreme Court ruled that

    a.   all laws protecting slavery were unconstitutional.
    b.   slavery was permissible in the South but northern states could prohibit slavery if they chose.
    c.   African Americans had no constitutional rights, and Congress could not prohibit slavery.
    d.   None of the above.

13. All of the following were used by southern states to disenfranchise black voters, except

    a.   property qualifications.
    b.   poll taxes.
    c.   literacy tests.
    d.   occupational tests.

14. The constitutional basis for the case outlawing segregated public schools was the

    a.   First Amendment freedom of speech clause.
    b.   equal protection clause of the Fourteenth Amendment.
    c.   right to vote provision of the Fifteenth Amendment.
    d.   necessary and proper clause of Article I, Section 8.

15. All of the following are examples of civil disobedience, except

    a. boycott of businesses.
    b. a protest march down the main street of a city.
    c. a sit-in at lunch counters.
    d. bomb threats of public facilities.

16. In the Bakke case, the Supreme Court ruled that

    a. set quotas in university admissions based solely on race were unconstitutional.
    b. set quotas of any kind were unconstitutional.
    c. quotas were acceptable if the applicants from majority groups did not protest.
    d. quotas were required in some circumstances.

17. According to the text, a major new development in the spread of white supremacist hate groups is the

    a. First Amendment protection of such groups.
    b. controversy of federal law enforcement efforts at Waco and Ruby Ridge.
    c. ease of communicating over the Internet.
    d. increase in TV talk shows.

18. The test of reasonableness

    a. was the traditional standard used by courts in sexual discrimination cases.
    b. was based on whether a reasonable person would agree that a law had a rational basis.
    c. made it very difficult to prove sexual discrimination.
    d. All of the above.

19. Who led the attack on the test of reasonableness?

    a. Sandra Day O'Connor   b. Thurgood Marshall
    c. Ruth Bader Ginsburg   d. Alan Dershowitz

20. The text states that American society will have to deal with questions of discrimination and equality with two other groups, which are

    a. Arabs and Asians.
    b. Muslims and Hindus.
    c. white males and the religious right.
    d. the elderly and homosexuals.

True or False

21.   T   F   Civil liberties are the constitutionally guaranteed rights of the individual that may not be removed arbitrarily by government.

22.   T   F   The 1857 Dred Scott case had far-reaching implications for the civil rights of women.

23.   T   F   The case known as Brown II ordered lower federal courts to enforce desegregation plans in public schools with all deliberate speed.

24.   T   F   The Civil Rights Act of 1964 greatly increased the federal governments ability to fight discrimination.

25.   T   F   A major complicating factor in trying to end racial discrimination in the North was segregation in the North was de facto, based on non-governmental factors and thus hard   to change by law.

26.   T   F   Following the 1969 case of *Alexander v. Holmes County Board of Education*, in which the Court ruled that every school district must desegregate immediately, the South became the most integrated schools in the nation but there was little progress in the northern cities.

27.   T   F   Removing legal obstacles does not automatically result in actual equality.

28.   T   F   Those in favor of affirmative action argue that because of the effects of past discrimination, true equality could not be achieved until those effects are overcome by transition programs giving minorities temporary advantages.

29.   T   F   The Clinton Administration's policy toward civil rights has been ambiguous, sometimes supporting past programs strongly and at other times calling for more study and review.

30.   T   F   The strict scrutiny test will make it much easier to uphold federal affirmative action programs.

Fill-in-the-Blanks

31.   The constitutionally guaranteed rights that may not be arbitrarily removed by the government, such as the right to vote, are called _____.

32.   Equality of results, or _____, measures whether real world obstacles to equal treatment exist.

33.   Equality before the law is called _____.

34.   _____ laws were passed by Southern states that separated the races in public places.

35.   A system in which employers advance wages and then require workers to remain on their jobs, in effect enslaving them, until the debt is satisfied is called _____.

36.   The elimination of laws and practices mandating separation of the races is called _____.

37.   When a person breaks the law in a nonviolent way and is willing to go to jail in order to publicly demonstrate that the law is unjust, that person is engaging in _____.

38.   When protestors refuse to patronize any organization that practices policies that are perceived to be unfair for political, economic, or ideological reasons, they are _____.

39.   _____ programs attempt to improve the chances of minority applicants for jobs, housing, employment, or graduate admissions by giving them a boost relative to white applicants with roughly the same qualifications.

40.   The idea that people should have equal rights and opportunities to develop their talents that all people should begin at the same starting point in a race defines _____.

Short Answer Essay

41.   Explain the difference between defacto equality and dejure equality.

42.   Explain the difference between desegregation and integration.

43.   Describe the Dred Scott case and its importance.

44.   Explain the difference between equality of result and equality of opportunity.

45.   Explain the difference between a strict scrutiny test and a heightened scrutiny test.

46.   Explain the Court's reasoning in the Brown v. Board of Education opinion. How did the different branches of federal government effect the implementation of this ruling?

47. Describe the major provisions of the Civil Rights Act of 1964 and the Voting Rights Act of 1965.

48. Give the forms of discrimination Americans with disabilities face and describe the actions of Congress in this area.

49. Trace the history of women's rights in America since the first Supreme Court case striking down sex discrimination.

50. Describe the kinds of discrimination experienced by Hispanic Americans.

Chapter Fifteen

Public Policy and Politics

Briefly define each of the following terms.

1. social welfare policy

2. policy elites

3. issue state

4. triggering mechanism

5. implementation

6. policy evaluation

7. environmental impact statement

8. means testing

9. poverty level

10. policy entrepreneurs

Multiple Choice

11. Which of the following is not an example of public policy?

    a. Regulating industry
    b. Achieving societal goals
    c. National defense
    d. Unifying religious organizations

12. Policy elites include:

    a. Members of Congress.
    b. The President.
    c. Leading influential columnist and commentators in the media.
    d. All of the above.

13. Who has the primary responsibility for the formulation and implementation of public policy?

    a. Congress   b. The Courts
    c. Federal agencies   d. All of the above

14. The largest single non-defense item in the national budget is

    a. public education.   b. social security.
    c. medical research.   d. congressional salaries.

15. Regulatory policies have
  a. increased in recent years.
  b. decreased in recent years.
  c. remained the same in recent years.
  d. been declared unconstitutional.

16. Pollution credits were created by
  a. the Kyoto Protocol.
  b. the Environmental Protection Act of 1960.
  c. the Clear Air Act of 1990.
  d. the Water Conservation Act of 1995.

17. The income tax is an example of a:
  a. flat tax.   b. value-added tax.
  c. progressive tax.   d. regressive tax.

18. Tax deductions that reduce the amount of income that is subject to taxes, such as home mortgages, are called
  a. tax revenues.   b. tax liabilities.
  c. tax shelters.   d. tax expenditures.

19. The key to budget resolution is two broad types of
  a. taxing.   b. spending.
  c. budgeting.   d. borrowing.

20. What type of government policy has the clearest impact on the economy?
  a. fiscal policy
  b. regulatory policy
  c. monetary policy
  d. international economic policy

True or False

21. T   F   Regulatory policy involves the use of police powers by the federal government.

22. T   F   The term logrolling refers to policies that benefit a particular state or district.

23. T   F   The national government may regulate the price charged for a good or service.

24. T   F   Social security is an example of an entitlement.

25. T   F   Social security recipients are subjected to means testing.

26. T   F   The World Trade Organization (WTO) promotes tariffs to protect the economies of member nations.

27. T   F   Capital gains tax comes mostly from lower-income taxpayers.

28. T   F   In general, the greater the number of tax brackets, the more progressive the tax.

29. T   F   The Clinton tax reform placed its emphasis on those with the greatest ability to pay.

30. T   F   When fully implemented in the next several years, NAFTA will make trade among the United States, Canada, and Mexico as free and easy as among the states across America.

Fill-in-the-Blanks

31. In contrast to _____, social welfare policy used positive incentives.

32. The _____ is the set of topics that are a source of concern for policy elites, the general public, or both.

33. American political history offers many examples of _____ _____ who succeeded in placing a potential policy issue on the public agenda.

34. Following evaluation, policies are either terminated or continued. If they are continued, they enter what social scientists call the _____ _____.

35. The Great Depression acted as a _____ _____ to translate the economic condition of poverty into a political issue to be addressed by policy makers.

36. The tax on unearned income from rents, stocks, and interest is called _____.

37. The annual shortfall between monies that the government takes in and spends is the _____.

38. The president's refusal to spend funds appropriated by Congress is called _____.

39. A statement passed by Congress that is the framework for spending decisions is called a _____.

40. _____ spending accounts for 33 percent of all federal spending and is the spending Congress actually controls.

Short Answer Essay

41. What are the four objectives of public policy?

42. Describe the policy life-cycle.

43. How does an issue become included in the formal agenda?

44. What is the Kyoto Protocol?

45. What are the characteristics of an effective public policy?

46. List and discuss the five aspects of policy making that make it a highly political process.

47. What are the three sets of concerns relating to future environmental regulation?

48. List the three primary goals of economic policy and explain the relationship among them.

49. Describe the political process of creating the federal budget.

50. Explain and give examples of uncontrollable expenditures.

Chapter Sixteen

Foreign Policy

Briefly define each of the following terms

1. foreign policy

2. Monroe Doctrine

3. superpower

4. North Atlantic Treaty Organization

5. bipolarity

6. foreign aid

7. Gulf of Tonkin Resolution

8. detente

9. economic sanctions

10. legislative oversight

Multiple Choice

11. All of the following are core goals of American foreign relations, except

    a. military security.
    b. isolationism.
    c. survival and independence.
    d. economic security.

12. During the post-World War II period, the term superpower applied

    a. only to the United States.
    b. both to the United Sates and the Soviet Union.
    c. to the western and communist alliance systems.
    d. to any nation that developed an atomic bomb.

13. The intention to assist free, democratic nations beat back the threat of totalitarianism became known as the

    a. Monroe Doctrine.
    b. Truman Doctrine.
    c. New World Order.
    d. War Powers Resolution.

14. The U.S. monopoly of nuclear weapons ended in

    a. 1914.
    b. 1945.
    c. 1949.
    d. 1990.

15. The Alliance For Progress program focused on

    a. Africa.
    b. Latin America.
    c. Eastern Europe.
    d. China.

16. The Gulf of Tonkin Resolution granted

    a. President Nixon authority to initiate a policy of detente.
    b. President Johnson authority to pursue the war in Vietnam.
    c. President Kennedy authority to invade Cuba.
    d. None of the above.

17. President Clinton's Partnership for Peace initiative was concerned with

    a. negotiating an end to nuclear proliferation under the auspices of the United States.
    b. strengthening NAFTA and expanding it to include other nations in Latin America.
    c. preventing Iraq from again invading Kuwait.
    d. increased military cooperation and integration as a first step toward NATO membership.

18. The Clinton administration tried to respond to the new global economic environment by stressing the policy of

    a. regionalism.   b. globalism.
    c. enlargement.   d. containment.

19. The oldest and most preeminent department of the foreign policy bureaucracy is considered to be the Department of

    a. State.   b. Defense.
    c. Commerce.   d. Justice.

20. The five core goals of U.S. foreign relations do not include:

    a. survival and independence.
    b. containment.
    c. military and economic security.
    d. territorial integrity.

True or False

21. T   F   The Monroe Doctrine reinforced isolationism by promising not to interfere in the internal concerns of European states.

22. T   F   The nuclear age began with the U.S. bombing of Hiroshima and Nagasaki in August 1945.

23. T   F   U.S.-imposed economic sanctions against Iraq, Haiti, Bosnia, Serbia, and Cuba have had their desired effect.

24. T F The president decides whether to receive ambassadors.

25. T F Presidents have generally ignored the reporting requirements of the War Powers Resolution.

26. T F The popularity of foreign aid programs has increased in the United States since the mid-70s.

27. T F Madeleine Albright is the first woman secretary of state and the highest ranking woman in government.

28. T F The CIA's most important function is paramilitary maneuvers.

29. T F Most Americans are well informed about foreign affairs.

30. T F Historically, American citizens have had little significant influence on the foreign policy created by their government.

Fill-in-the-Blanks

31. A pattern in which the United States fosters economic relations abroad without committing to strategic alliances that might draw the country into a war is called _____.

32. The view in which the U.S. sphere of influence has expanded beyond the Western Hemisphere to include virtually every corner of the globe where U.S. interests might be affected is called _____.

33. The disproportionate power that distinguished the United States and the Soviet Union from all other countries in the postwar era defines _____.

34. U.S. foreign policy after 1946 was guided by the doctrine of _____, a concept delineated by George Kennan, then a State Department Soviet expert.

35. The bipolar struggle between the United States and the Soviet Union that began in the 1950s and ended in the 1990s was known as the _____.

36. The _____ was a treaty signed by the Soviet Union and the eastern bloc in Europe agreeing to mutual defense, in reaction to NATO.

37. Richard Nixon initiated a policy of _____ in an attempt to relax the tensions between the United States and the Soviet Union through limited cooperation.

38. The _____ was signed by the United States (under President Nixon) and the Soviet Union to limit various classes of nuclear weapons.

39. The power that Congress has to oversee the operation of various federal agencies is called _____.

40. President Eisenhower in 1961 called the growing power and influence resulting from the conjunction of an immense military establishment and a large arms industry the _____.

Short Answer

41. Explain the paradoxes of the concept of national interest.

42. Describe the significant events occurring during the first era of U.S. foreign policy.

43. Describe the significant events occurring during the second era of U.S. foreign policy.

44. Describe the development of U.S. foreign policy from the end of the World War II to detente.

45. Describe the important foreign policy issues since the breakup of the Soviet Union.

46. Explain the difference between the International Security Assistance Force and the United Nations Peacekeeping forces.

47. Explain why the president has become preeminent in foreign affairs.

48. Describe the constraints on Congress' ability to influence foreign policy.

49. List examples of Congress' impact on foreign policy through oversight.

50. Explain how the press and public opinion can act as a check on foreign-policy outcomes.

Answer Key

Chapter 1	Chapter 2	Chapter 3	Chapter 4
Multiple Choice	**Multiple Choice**	**Multiple Choice**	**Multiple Choice**
11. C	11. C	11. A	11. A
12. D	12. B	12. B	12. A
13. C	13. B	13. D	13. C
14. D	14. C	14. C	14. B
15. A	15. A	15. D	15. C
16. B	16. B	16. D	16. D
17. D	17. B	17. C	17. D
18. C	18. C	18. C	18. B
19. B	19. D	19. B	19. A
20. C	20. A	20. A	20. C
True/False	**True/False**	**True/False**	**True/False**
21. F	21. T	21. F	21. F
22. F	22. F	22. T	22. T
23. T	23. F	23. F	23. F
24. T	24. F	24. F	24. F
25. F	25. F	25. T	25. T
26. T	26. T	26. T	26. F
27. T	27. F	27. T	27. T
28. T	28. F	28. T	28. T
29. F	29. T	29. T	29. F
30. T	30. T	30. T	30. F
Fill-in-blank	**Fill-in-blank**	**Fill-in-blank**	**Fill-in-blank**
31. direct democracy	31. bicameral legislature	31. states rights	31. necessary and proper
32. town meeting	32. legislative branch (or legislature)	32. triad of powers	32. reapportionment
33. political discussion	33. limited government	33. carrot and stick	33. redistricting
34. negative freedom	34. Townsend Revenue Acts	34. supremacy	34. trustees
35. order, stability	35. Articles of Confederation	35. reserved powers	35. incumbents
36. shifting alliances	36. Social contract	36. police powers	36. term limits
37. political parties	37. Electoral College System	37. nullification	37. two congresses
38. elections	38. Federalism	38. incorporation	38. subcommittees
39. right to privacy	39. Bill of Rights	39. federal mandate	39. log rolling
40. totalitarianism	40. Democratic	40. special revenue sharing	40. congressional agenda

Answer Key

Chapter 5	Chapter 6	Chapter 7	Chapter 8
Multiple Choice	**Multiple Choice**	**Multiple Choice**	**Multiple Choice**
11. B	11. D	11. D	11. C
12. A	12. C	12. C	12. A
13. A	13. D	13. D	13. A
14. A	14. D	14. B	14. C
15. B	15. C	15. D	15. B
16. D	16. D	16. A	16. D
17. A	17. C	17. D	17. D
18. B	18. C	18. C	18. A
19. B	19. D	19. C	19. B
20. B	20. D	20. A	20. D
True/False	**True/False**	**True/False**	**True/False**
21. T	21. T	21. T	21. T
22. T	22. T	22. F	22. F
23. F	23. F	23. T	23. F
24. T	24. F	24. F	24. F
25. T	25. T	25. T	25. T
26. T	26. T	26. T	26. T
27. T	27. T	27. F	27. T
28. T	28. F	28. T	28. F
29. F	29. T	29. F	29. T
30. T	30. T	30. T	30. F
Fill-in-blank	**Fill-in-blank**	**Fill-in-blank**	**Fill-in-blank**
31. electoral college	31. appelate	31. independent regulatory commissions	31. representative sample
32. treaties	32. trial (or petit) court	32. formal rules	32. question wording
33. executive agreements	33. class action	33. welfare state	33. tracking polls
34. rally effect	34. senatorial courtesy	34. spoils system	34. straw poll
35. stewardship	35. docket	35. civil service	35. television
36. constructionist	36. rule of four	36. implementation	36. conservative
37. veto	37. opinion	37. cabinet departments	37. liberty
38. War Powers Resolution	38. dissenting opinion	38. iron triangles	38. political ideology
39. chief of staff	39. stare decisis	39. senior executive service	39. schema
40. vice president	40. judicial activism	40. The Office of Management & Budget	40. intensity

Answer Key

Chapter 9	Chapter 10	Chapter 11
Multiple Choice	**Multiple Choice**	**Multiple Choice**
11. D	11. B	11. C
12. A	12. A	12. C
13. C	13. B	13. C
14. B	14. A	14. A
15. B	15. C	15. C
16. A	16. C	16. B
17. A	17. A	17. D
18. A	18. C	18. A
19. A	19. C	19. D
20. A	20. D	20. D
True/False	**True/False**	**True/False**
21. T	21. F	21. T
22. T	22. T	22. T
23. T	23. F	23. F
24. T	24. F	24. F
25. F	25. F	25. T
26. T	26. F	26. F
27. F	27. F	27. F
28. T	28. T	28. T
29. F	29. T	29. F
30. F	30. F	30. F
Fill-in-blank	**Fill-in-blank**	**Fill-in-blank**
31. political parties	31. poll tax	31. diffusing
32. Revolution of 1800	32. voter turnout	32. collective action
33. recruitment	33. initiative	33. public interest group
34. primary system	34. straight party	34. single issue
35. machine politics	35. retrospective voting	35. maintenance
36. party platform	36. mid-term elections	36. access
37. winner-take-all system	37. faithless elector	37. direct mail
38. closed	38. maintaining election	38. lobbying
39. superdelegate	39. soft money	39. soft money
40. electoral college	40. independent expenditures	40. David Truman

Answer Key

Chapter 12	Chapter 13	Chapter 14
Multiple Choice	**Multiple Choice**	**Multiple Choice**
11. C	11. C	11. A
12. B	12. B	12. C
13. A	13. C	13. D
14. D	14. C	14. B
15. A	15. A	15. D
16. B	16. C	16. A
17. C	17. C	17. C
18. C	18. C	18. D
19. D	19. D	19. C
20. B	20. B	20. D
True/False	**True/False**	**True/False**
21. F	21. T	21. F
22. T	22. F	22. F
23. F	23. T	23. T
24. F	24. F	24. T
25. F	25. F	25. T
26. F	26. T	26. T
27. T	27. T	27. T
28. F	28. T	28. T
29. F	29. T	29. T
30. T	30. T	30. F
Fill-in-blank	**Fill-in-blank**	**Fill-in-blank**
31. right of rebuttal	31. incorporation	31. civil rights
32. liberal media elite	32. clear and present danger	32. defacto equality
33. investigative journalism	33. double jeopardy	33. dejure equality
34. socialization	34. Lemon	34. Jim Crow
35. surveillance, interpretation, investigative journalism, and socialization.	35. secular regulation	35. peonage
36. fairness doctrine	36. fighting words	36. desegregation
37. prior restraint	37. hate speech	37. civil disobedience
38. symbiotic	38. symbolic speech	38. boycotting
39. horse race	39. prior restraint	39. affirmative action
40. sound bites	40. Miranda	40. equality of opportunity

Answer Key

Chapter 15	Chapter 16
Multiple Choice	**Multiple Choice**
11. D	11. B
12. D	12. B
13. D	13. B
14. B	14. C
15. A	15. B
16. C	16. B
17. C	17. D
18. D	18. C
19. B	19. A
20. A	20. B
True/False	**True/False**
21. T	21. T
22. F	22. T
23. T	23. F
24. T	24. T
25. F	25. T
26. F	26. F
27. F	27. T
28. T	28. F
29. T	29. F
30. T	30. T
Fill-in-blank	**Fill-in-blank**
31. regulatory policy	31. isolationism
32. policy agenda	32. globalism
33. policy entrepreneur	33. superpower
34. feedback loop	34. containment
35. triggering mechanism	35. cold war
36. capital gains tax	36. Warsaw Pact
37. deficit	37. détente
38. impoundment	38. Strategic Arms Limitation Treaty
39. budget regulation	39. legislative oversight
40. discretionary	40. military-industrial complex